THE DISCIPLES CONCLUSION

Dr. Aaron R. Jones

THE DISCIPLES CONCLUSION

Copyright © 2015 by Dr. Aaron R. Jones

Printed in the United States of America

Published by Kingdom Kaught Publishing LLC, Denton, Maryland

All rights reserved. No part of this book may be reproduced or transmitted in any form or by any means, electronic or mechanical, including photocopying, recording or by any information storage and retrieval system without written permission of the author, except for the inclusion of brief quotations in a review. All scripture quotations are from the King James Version of the Bible. Thomas Nelson Publishers, Nashville: Thomas Nelson, Inc. 1972.

Editor: Sharon Jones

Copy-editing: Sarah Gardner

Graphic Designers Support: Cartia Brown-Morgan, Juanita Bank and Reneto Gordon

Jesus at the Treasury and Seashore images by ©SuperStock/Masterfile

Disciple's Ponder image by Stefano Mortellora (Attribution 2.0 Generic; CC BY 2.0)

ISBN 978-0-9961267-0-0

Library of Congress Control Number: 2015903603

Acknowledgments

First I would like to thank my Lord and Savior Jesus Christ, who has blessed me with the talents, the skills, and the abilities to reach this point in my life.

A special thanks to my loving wife, Sharon, who has always given her love, time, and support in all of my projects. Without her support, this project could not have been completed.

I also would like to thank Nita Washington, my Book Manager; Cartia Brown-Morgan and Reneto Gordon for their graphics assistance on this project.

The Lord has truly blessed me with a good supportive team.

Table of Contents

INTRODUCTION | 1

CONCLUSION | 5
Must make Jesus the #1 priority

CONCLUSION | 15
Must stay on the path

CONCLUSION | 27
Must count the price (cost)

CONCLUSION | 35
Must not cling to earthly possessions

CONCLUSION | 43
Must be productive

CONCLUSION | 55
Must have passion

CONCLUSION | 65
Must know his position

CONCLUSION | 73
Must be willing to press

CONCLUSION | 83
Must be prepared to forgive

CONCLUSION | 93
Must be one of prayer

CONCLUSION | 103
Must have positive obedience

CONCLUSION | 113
Must have a purged heart

CONCLUSION | 121
Must fulfill the Great Commission

INTRODUCTION

Every day the world is creating disciples. The people in the world follow what makes them feel happy and good, regardless of the consequences. The world presents a powerful influence. We are called to be followers, but not followers of this world. A disciple by definition is one who is a learner and a follower.

Jesus chose certain men to be followers of Him, and He trained them to build the Kingdom of God. The twelve men Jesus chose had the assignment to be witnesses for Him. The twelve were not only called disciples, but also apostles. Matthew 10:2-4 identifies all twelve disciples:

"Now the names of the twelve apostles are these; The first, Simon, who is called Peter, and Andrew his broth-

er; James the son of Zebedee, and John his brother; Philip, and Bartholomew; Thomas, and Matthew the publican; James the son of Alphaeus, and Lebbaeus, whose surname was Thaddaeus; Simon the Canaanite, and Judas Iscariot, who also betrayed him."

What makes the chosen twelve so powerful is that they were not superstars; they were ordinary men. Jesus is not looking for Christian superheroes, but for men and women who will be obedient and faithful disciples. More importantly, He is looking for those who will allow the power of the Holy Spirit to use them in an extraordinary way. Although the disciples were used after the resurrection and the in-filling of the Holy Ghost, the Bible does reveal their weaknesses in ministry.

The call to be a disciple is the greatest call of the believer, because it crosses all paths of ministry. If we want to do great things for God, we must embrace the strategic call as followers of

INTRODUCTION

Jesus. Every born-again believer is called to be a disciple of Jesus.

Once we identify ourselves as disciples of Jesus Christ, we strive daily to live by His words and teachings. The heart of Jesus has always been for souls and the Kingdom of God. Jesus provided the example (Himself) and clear instructions of what it takes to be a disciple of God.

Those who are willing to accept the call as a disciple of Jesus Christ are strengthened by the Holy Spirit. During Jesus' ministry on earth, He took the time to pour Himself into the disciples (the twelve chosen men). The disciples were with Jesus morning and night. They ate, slept, and ministered together.

Before we can make disciples, as Jesus commanded, I truly believe we must understand what it means to be a disciple. In the Gospels,

Jesus does not leave any room for gray areas in the roles of disciples. A disciple of Jesus understands that obedience to His Word is a command of God; a challenge from God; and a changed lifestyle for God.

As followers of Jesus Christ, we are soldiers in His army. Any military soldier understands the consequences for not obeying and following the orders of his commander. A soldier will embrace a mission that he doesn't understand, and will follow the orders, even unto death. As disciples and soldiers for Jesus Christ, we have a great calling. Not only are human lives at stake, but eternal lives, as well. In this book, I will identify the roles of a disciple and how Jesus addresses each role in clear and emphatic language.

CONCLUSION 1

Jesus Must Be the #1 Priority

"If any man come to me, and hate not his father, and mother, and wife, and children, and brethren, and sisters, yea, and his own life also, he cannot be my disciple."
Luke 14:26

One of the hardest assignments of a disciple is keeping Jesus as number One (always). The core problem in fulfilling this role or conclusion is found in Mark 4:19.

"...the cares of this world, and the deceitfulness of riches, and the lusts of other things entering in, choke the word, and it becometh unfruitful."

Jesus lists three things that keep Him from being a number one priority in our lives and daily Christian walk. Care of the world, deceitfulness, and lust have the power to choke what He deposits in us. We cannot allow life and the world to take over and consume us. We cannot allow these things to replace Him in our hearts. Jesus should always hold the highest place in our lives. Jesus should be in the center of our hearts. Being in the center means His words and ways call the shots.

When Jesus is the center of our hearts; He reigns and is in control. When Jesus is not first, there is no other option but for sin to reign. The apostle Paul says clearly in Romans 6:12, *"Let not sin reign in your mortal body, that you should obey the lust."* Paul is explaining how flesh can be the number one priority in one's life, and it will influence one's decisions. This is why Romans 8:5 is important:

CONCLUSION 1

"For they that are after the flesh do mind the things of the flesh; but they that are after the Spirit the things of the Spirit."

We must follow after the Spirit to keep Jesus first. When we follow after the Spirit, the flesh is not a priority.

As part of making Jesus the number One priority in our lives; we must be able to balance our daily relationships. Jesus made known that family and friend relationships are not to come before Him and His Kingdom assignments. These relationships cannot take precedence over the relationship we have with Him. The moment we allow any other relationship to become our number one priority, we cannot serve Jesus to our fullest potential. Yes, we have the responsibility to take care of our families and establish friendships. However, when God calls the disciple for an assignment, small or big, he must be ready and accessible. If the disciple is not careful, he will use family and friends as an excuse not to be obedient to orders given by the Heavenly Father.

Jesus marks the standard for placing Him first. Jesus says in Matthew 6:33, *"But seek ye first the kingdom of God, and his righteousness; and all these things shall be added unto you."* This is the clearest principle to keeping Jesus first. When we seek the Kingdom, we are seeking His righteousness; and when we are seeking His righteousness, we are seeking the Kingdom. The idea of seeking is a continuous action. Keeping Jesus as the #1 priority must involve a constant search for Him and His Kingdom. The act of putting Jesus as #1 has a promise connected to it, *"…and all these things will be given to you as well."*

The context of Matthew 6:33 is the Father's ability to take care of His children's basic needs (food, clothing, and shelter). Jesus says in Matthew 6:31, 32:

CONCLUSION 1

"Therefore take no thought saying, What shall we eat? Or, What shall we drink? Or, Wherewithal shall we be clothed. (For after all these things do the Gentiles, seek:) for your heavenly Father knoweth that ye have need of all these things."

At times, our basic needs become a hindrance because we have placed the flesh as our first priority. Jesus assists in this area with His comforting words; and I paraphrase, "Take care of My business and I will take care of yours."

Our priority to have Jesus as number One must be intentional and desired. We must learn daily to ask Him for wisdom on how to balance the challenges of life, so that He remains number One in all things.

Another important element in keeping Jesus first is never losing the joy of your first love. In Revelation chapter 2, Jesus has an issue with the Church of Ephesus. Although it did a lot of things right, it did one important thing wrong: the congregation left their first love. As disciples, we can function in the church and still lose our first love. In other words, the church was going through the motions, but Jesus was not the #1 priority.

"I know thy works, and thy labour, and thy patience, and how thou canst not bear them which are evil: and thou hast tried them which say they are apostles, and are not, and hast found them liars: And hast borne, and hast patience, and for my name's sake hast labored, and hast not fainted. "Nevertheless I have somewhat against thee, because thou hast left thy first love" (verses 2-4).

The first and only eternal love we have ever experienced is the love of our Lord and Savior Jesus Christ. Daily, we must stay in love with He Who Is and the Kingdom He represents. Throughout the Bible, the love of Christ is expressed and displayed.

CONCLUSION 1

What have I placed before Jesus?

What has taken my attention away from my Kingdom assignment?

What must I add in and subtract from my life so that Jesus can remain as my #1 priority?

THE DISCIPLES CONCLUSION

Dear Lord,

Help me to remove the things I have placed in my life that are stopping You from being my #1 priority. Please reveal those things that are separating me from my Kingdom assignments. I ask for Your wisdom, right now, so that I may be able to identify the secrets things that I have hid in my heart. I need Your Spirit to continue to challenge my heart that you may always, and at all times, be first in my life.

Amen

CONCLUSION 1

CONCLUSION 2

Must Stay On the Path (Journey)

"And whosoever doth not bear his cross, and come after me cannot be my disciple."
Luke 14:27

In many ways, life is about multiple journeys with diverse paths. Many of life's journeys are based on decisions we have made to direct and influence our paths. Many people do not realize that we can do all the right things and still follow the wrong path. Many people spend most of their money, time, and effort in journeys God has not ordained for their lives. Quite often, the paths we choose to take can seem right in our own eyes. Proverbs 16:25 says, *"There is a way that seemeth right unto a man, but the end thereof are the ways of death."* As a disciple, we cannot only rely on what seems right; but we must also rely on where God tells us to go.

Jesus provides the path floor plans of the right and the wrong ways for His disciples. Jesus says in Matthew 7:13, 14, *"Enter ye in at the strait gate: for wide is the gate, and broad is the way, that leadeth to destruction, and many there be which go in thereat: Because strait is the gate, and narrow is the way, which leadeth unto life, and few there be that find it."* When we take the wide gate there will always be a broader path. What that simply means is you will have more available options to keep going in the wrong direction. When we take the straight gate, the options are limited to one direction and that is to Jesus Christ Himself.

The Bible is clear in the direction of where a disciple should go. There is only one path that guarantees eternal life. John 14:6 says, *"Jesus saith unto him, I am the way, the truth, and the life: no man cometh unto the Father, but by me."*

There is only one way to the Father and that is through Jesus Christ. This is the path of the disciple. One of the strategies of the enemy is to constantly make other paths available and enticing. The enemy will make sure all available options are made known to you. He doesn't believe you want to be a disciple so much that you will not entertain other paths in life. His distractions are to cause you to lose focus. Disciples cannot afford to lose focus while entertaining the distractions of Satan. Satan's assignment is to get the disciple off the path with his deception. Remember, Satan has developed weapons to weaken your focus and hinder your walk with Jesus.

When Satan comes to pull you off track, use Jesus' example found in Matthew 4:1-11. Each time Satan attempted to pull Jesus off track, He responded to Satan with the Word of God.

"Then was Jesus led up of the Spirit into the wilderness to be tempted of the devil. And when he had fasted forty days and forty nights, he was afterward an hungred. And when the tempter came to him, he said, "If thou be the Son of God, command that these stones be made bread." But he answered and said, "It is written, Man shall not live by bread alone, but by every word that proceedeth out of the mouth of God." Then the devil taketh him up into the holy city, and setteth him on a pinnacle of the temple, And saith unto him, "If thou be the Son of God, cast thyself down: for it is written, He shall give his angels charge concerning thee: and in their hands they shall bear thee up, lest at any time thou dash thy foot against a stone." Jesus said unto him, "It is written again, Thou shalt not tempt the Lord thy God." Again, the devil taketh him up into an exceeding high mountain, and sheweth him all the kingdoms of the world, and the glory of them; And saith unto him, "All these things will I give thee, if thou wilt fall down and worship me." Then saith Jesus unto him, "Get thee

hence, Satan: for it is written, Thou shalt worship the Lord thy God, and him only shalt thou serve." Then the devil leaveth him, and, behold, angels came and ministered unto him."

Jesus in each attempt stated, "It Is Written," to prevent losing focus and getting off track. Jesus gave Satan the one thing he could not beat, The Word of God. In like manner, when Satan is tempting you with fleshly things, you must also fight back with the Word of God. The Word is the weapon for Satan's "knock you off the path" attacks.

In order to stay on the path, the disciple's eyes must stay on Jesus. Psalm 121:1 says, *"I will lift up mine eyes unto the hills, from whence cometh my help."* Your trust must be in the Father. You must trust Him to see you through all circumstances and situations.

THE DISCIPLES CONCLUSION

Once we become a disciple of Jesus Christ, turning back should not be an option. Our confession becomes "I will not turn back." Once you make that decision, no matter how trouble comes, you are moving forward. I am reminded of an airplane ride. Oftentimes on plane rides, there is turbulence that makes for a very uncomfortable and nervous flight. We know, in most cases, a few things: (1) the turbulence is normally for a block of time; (2) the pilot sees or is aware of the possible turbulence; (3) the pilot has experience in dealing with the turbulence; and (4) the pilot informs us of turbulence and tells us that we will go through in order to reach our destination. Yes, we pray, but in the natural we are trusting to a degree that the pilot will get us to our destination with Divine support.

Now, if we can trust a pilot to get us through turbulence while flying, surely we can trust the One who has complete control of our destiny.

CONCLUSION 2

God will be there through all turbulent times. Don't leave the path at the sign of turbulence. Trust God through the turbulence.

To remain on the path, the disciple must understand that the distraction will pass away. We must say goodbye forever to past thoughts, ways, and opinions. One of the challenges in our Christian walk is the temptation to go back to the past in order to deal with the future. II Corinthians 5:17 says, *"Therefore if any man be in Christ, he is a new creature: old things are passed away; behold, all things are become new."*

As a disciple, we cannot have a "Stop following Jesus" clause. To bear the cross of Jesus, we cannot be self-centered and have a self-agenda. We must be about God's agenda. We must stay focused and look forward. Looking back gives way for stopping God's agenda. Everyone has their own cross and that is the cross he must carry. A disciple's step is ordered and ordained from the beginning of time. Ephesians 1:3, 4 says, *"Blessed be the God and Father of our Lord Jesus Christ, who hath blessed us with all spiritual blessings in heavenly places in Christ: According as he hath chosen us in him before the foundation of the world, that we should be holy and without blame before him in love."* Understanding this, a disciple will purpose in his heart to stay on the path God has predestined for him.

CONCLUSION 2

Do I have a "Stop following Jesus" clause?

Are my decisions controlling my path in a negative way?

What is my response to the enemy when turbulent times arise?

THE DISCIPLES CONCLUSION

Dear Lord,

Keep me on Your path. Give me more wisdom to identify all of Satan's distractions to lead me in another direction. Allow me to always carry the cross You have given me. If there is any desire to quit in me, please remove it now. Strengthen my trust in you during the turbulent times.

Amen

CONCLUSION 2

CONCLUSION

Must Count the Price (Cost)

"For which of you, intending to build a tower, sitteth not down first, and counteth the cost, whether he have sufficient to finish it?
Luke 14:28

In any gain, there is a loss. A wise disciple will count the cost in everything he does. Life is about counting the cost. We must count the cost with an open mind and spirit. As Jesus is soon to come back for His church, I believe that kingdom increase should be the motivation to count the cost. In ministry, we should always be obedient to God. In this obedience, we must always count the cost to ensure that we are in line with His Word. God wants the disciple to make counting the cost a part of his daily lifestyle. Being a disciple for Jesus Christ and the kingdom should be a win-win situation.

What should encourage every disciple is that Jesus counted the cost of the cross. He knew the greatest value of the cross was the souls of all mankind reuniting back to the Father. Even though, Jesus knew all of my failures and shortcomings, I rejoice in knowing that He looked at the cross and thought of me. Although He knew the pain and suffering He would endure, He still said, "yes." It is such a humbling thought that my life and redemption was worth the greatest sacrifice known to man.

In the view of eternity, following Jesus will always cost a disciple something and it is always worth it. Romans 8:18 says, *"For I reckon that the sufferings of this present time are not worthy to be compared with the glory which shall be revealed in us."* The difficult time for a disciple is getting past some of the present realities and trusting God for the future. A disciple must constantly remind himself, "This fight is worth the cost."

Many disciples want a great measure of anointing. They want God to use them mightily, but never imagine the cost involved. A disciple must keep in mind, "The more God uses him, the larger the enemy's target is on him." There is a sad commentary to God using men and women in powerful ways for the kingdom. The commentary is that many people desire the attention, but do not want to pay the price of having that attention. It is often said, "A person never really knows the cost of the anointing in a disciple's life." My advice to all disciples is to never covet the glory of another's ministry unless you can endure the price of living their story.

Many disciples know that following Jesus will cost them, but they try to get around the cost. I love the mentality of David. He made a very profound statement in 2 Samuel 24:24, *"And the king said unto Araunah, Nay; but I will surely buy it of thee at a price: neither will I offer burnt offerings unto the* LORD *my God of that which doth cost me nothing. So David bought the threshingfloor and the oxen for fifty shekels of silver."* David did not want to give anything to God that did not cost him anything. To some, this verse sounds crazy. Some even may ask, "Why count the cost if you don't have to?" Every sacrifice to God should have a piece of you in it. I believe there is more intensity and appreciation in a sacrifice that costs you something. When we count the cost, we understand that we will lose something in the sacrifice.

All loss is not a bad loss, and all gain is not a good gain. Matthew 16:26 says, *"For what is a man profited, if he shall gain the whole world, and lose his own soul? or what shall a man give in exchange for his soul?"*

When we count the cost, it will help us to stop making commitments and then quitting on God. There is so much unfinished work in the Kingdom because disciples do not count the cost. The tragedy is that some disciples take it lightly, but winning souls for the Kingdom depends on finishing the work. When we don't count the cost, sometimes souls suffer. When we count the cost, we must know that Jesus is the Source of the resource.

THE DISCIPLES CONCLUSION

What cost have I counted since I came to the Lord?

Does my worship cost me anything?

What will I lose? Am I ready to lose it for the Kingdom?

CONCLUSION 3

Dear Lord,

Help me to count the cost, so that I am in line with Your Word and plan for my life. Let me not take lightly any assignment for Your Kingdom. Forgive me Lord for any souls that were lost or hindered because I did not count the cost. Let my sacrifices cost me something.

Amen

THE DISCIPLES CONCLUSION

CONCLUSION 4

Must Not Cling to Earthly Possessions

"So likewise, whosoever he be of you that forsaketh not all that he hath, he cannot by my disciple"
Luke 14:33

We live in a world that is possession hungry. The world has made life about what a person can obtain. The world has used possessions to determine and define one's worth. There is a mindset, "The more possessions one has, the more power and influence he has." This mentality has made its way into the church of Jesus Christ.

We think a person is truly blessed by the amount of possessions he obtains. Some even believe the greater anointing is on those with more possessions. On the other hand, if one is limited in his or her possessions then he or she must lack faith, is cursed, or just not blessed. Yes, possessions have their place in our lives and God does desire to bless His children. But a disciple cannot allow possessions to dictate God's anointing, influence, power, or status of anyone.

Before I go any further, I want to put possessions in their proper place. Jesus states in Matthew 24:35, *"Heaven and earth shall pass away, but my words shall not pass away."* Everything that is not connected to God's Word is temporary and will pass away.

Jesus is the best gift ever known to man. Jesus is The Gift that keeps on giving. The world's temporary possessions are a major challenge in the Christian walk of a disciple. The strong desire to have material things can hinder one's effectiveness in the Kingdom. A disciple's connectivity to his possessions can cause worship of those possessions.

The parable of the rich man presents a real story of the struggle with temporary possessions.

"And a certain ruler asked him, saying, "Good Master, what shall I do to inherit eternal life?" And Jesus said unto him, "Why callest thou me good? none is good, save one, that is, God. Thou knowest the commandments, Do not commit adultery, Do not kill, Do not steal, Do not bear false witness, Honour thy father and thy mother." And he said, "All these have I kept from my youth up." Now when Jesus heard these things, he said unto him, "Yet lackest thou one thing: sell all that thou hast, and distribute unto the poor, and thou shalt have treasure in heaven: and come, follow me" (Luke 18:18-22).

There is nothing wrong with possessions, but possessions that consume the focus can become hindrances. Often, we live above our means and must work harder and longer to maintain our possessions. Christians often make work an excuse for not being committed to ministry, which is an honest assessment, but many times the work that must be done is because of wants/desires and not necessarily needs.

There shouldn't be any possessions in life that come before us and our relationship with Jesus. Oftentimes disciples want something from Jesus, but they aren't ready to separate from some of their possessions. No matter what God gives us, we should be ready at any given time to release it for the benefit of His Kingdom. The moment we try to hold on to our possessions, we miss something in God. If we cannot let a possession go; we must have a tight hold on it, or it has a tight hold on us.

CONCLUSION 4

The apostle Paul put the idea of money in its proper perspective. He writes in 1Timothy 6:10, *"...for the love of money is the root of all evil..."* It is not the possession of money that is evil, but the love of it makes it evil. When we put our money and possessions before God, it challenges our role as disciples. Be aware that any possession can be a disciple's god.

THE DISCIPLES CONCLUSION

What possessions in my life have a bigger hold on me than Jesus Christ?

What possessions do I want? Now compare them to what I need.

Can I release my possessions in order to fulfill God's greater plan?

CONCLUSION 4

Dear Lord,

Thank You for all the blessings You have given me and my family. All that I have is because of Your Hand in my life. Help me not place anything before You. Teach me to use wisdom and hear Your Voice as I deal with my possessions. Holy Spirit, be a constant reminder of my priorities.

Amen

THE DISCIPLES CONCLUSION

CONCLUSION

A Disciple Must Be Productive

"Herein is my Father glorified, that ye bear much fruit; so shall ye be my disciples."
John 15:8

Reproduction should be in the mind of every disciple. The role of every disciple is to make more disciples. Being a vessel for God should be the life of every disciple. This vessel should produce fruit, and more fruit. God is intentional about fruit bearing. God says two things He will do in John 15 regarding fruit bearing: He will prune and He will pluck. Jesus in John 15 says, *"...and every branch that beareth fruit, he purgeth it, that it may bring forth more fruit."*

As a disciple when you are not bearing fruit, God must do something; because the role of the disciple is to be productive and bear fruit. John 15:2 says, *"...that beareth not fruit he taketh away."* The best way I understand this verse is that the disciple has the benefit of eternal life, but is no longer a part of the plan. God lifts him from the tree. The disciple is a branch, and God expects every productive branch to bear fruit.

Purging Process

Purging is so that the disciple can bear more fruit. Purging is necessary for the growth of the Kingdom. Sometimes, we don't understand or like the purging process. To purge brings the understanding of cutting, God must cut, so we can grow and produce. God's cutting should not be looked upon as a negative. It is a positive to maximize His Kingdom.

Plucking Process

In any business, organization, or group when there are individuals who are not being productive, something is done. A CEO, manager, or supervisor will not tolerate non-productive employees. When non- productive behavior takes place, there are procedures that follow to deal with this behavior. If the corporate world deals with the lack of productivity with consequences, should we not expect an Almighty God to hold His disciples accountable to the productivity of His Kingdom. So, the plucking process is to make room for those who will be productive. God doesn't want good fruit to be non-productive fruit. As a disciple if you are not being productive, you are being a weight. God wants, the most productive disciples operating at all times.

As a disciple, in order to be productive, we must depend on the vine (Jesus). We cannot do anything outside of Jesus Christ. In order to bear fruit, you must abide in the vine (Jesus). Without the abiding, there is no righteousness, power, anointing, relationship, fellowship, or vitality. The more we allow God to purge us, the more we will be dependent on God. The biggest factor to a disciple's productivity is how he abides with the vine (Jesus). Jesus said in John 15:4, 5, *"Abide in me, and I in you. As the branch cannot bear fruit of itself, except it abide in the vine; no more can ye, except ye abide in me. I am the vine, ye are the branches: He that abideth in me, and I in him, the same bringeth forth much fruit: for without me ye can do nothing."*

God must be the Source of ministry and the fruit-bearing result. Oftentimes, much ministry is done without God's blessings. We should not put a limit on the fruit. Bearing fruit should be the drive to bear more fruit. God doesn't want us to be satisfied with just fruit, but MUCH

FRUIT. The disciple needs to be focused on much fruit!

Much fruit comes out of a constant connection with Jesus. The key word to connecting is abiding. Abide means to remain and dwell. We must understand that God has, from the beginning of time, wanted to dwell with His people. Two scriptures in the book of Exodus emphasize this point. Exodus 25:8 says, *"And let them make me a sanctuary; that I may dwell among them."* Exodus 29:45 says, *"And I will dwell among the children of Israel, and will be their God."* God wanted communion with Adam, but Adam sinned and destroyed the communion. Productivity encourages God's dwelling and communing with His people.

When we think of productivity, we must think of salt. When we operate as salt, we will be productive disciples. We know salt to be a preservative and can help the healing process of cuts and scrapes. As being the salt of the earth, disciples become the examples needed to build the Kingdom of God. In Matthew 5:14, Jesus provided the result of non-productive salt:

"Ye are the salt of the earth, but if the salt has lost its savor, wherewith it be salted? Thenceforth it is good for nothing but to be cast out, and to be trodden under the foot of men."

When we are totally committed as a disciple, we (like salt) are profitable for Kingdom building. Once we are salt, we must remain salty. We must ensure that we are just as effective through the Holy Spirit.

Jesus gives us a very disturbing diagnosis when we don't remain salty. When we lose our savor, we become disciples without any benefit to the Kingdom. And if we are unable to support Kingdom planting, Jesus calls us useless.

CONCLUSION 5

Our productivity has two main focuses: 1) to give glory to God and 2) to expand the Kingdom. I will discuss the expansion of the Kingdom in a later conclusion. The productivity is to bring glory to God... not to the disciple. John 15:8 says, *"Herein is my Father glorified, that ye bear much fruit; so shall ye be my disciples."* The more productive a disciple is the more glory goes to God. The truth of the matter is everything we do should bring glory to God. The apostle Paul emphasizes this truth in 1 Corinthians 10:31, *"Whether therefore ye eat, or drink, or whatsoever ye do, do all to the glory of God."*

As important as it is for disciples to bear fruit and glorify God; it is equally important for each disciple to assess himself. How effective and obedient is he to the call to be productive? The assessment involves three simple questions:

1. Am I conforming more like Jesus every day?

"But now being made free from sin, and become servants to God, ye have our fruit unto holiness, and end everlasting life." (Romans 6:22)

2. Am I having a consistent burden for lost souls like Jesus?

"The Lord is not slack concerning his promise, as some men count slackness; but is longsuffering to us-ward, not willing that any should perish, but that all should come to repentance." (2 Peter 3:9)

3. Am I behaving like Jesus?

"But the fruit of the Spirit is love, joy, peace, longsuffering, gentleness, goodness, faith, Meekness, temperance: against such there is no law." (Galatians 5:22, 23)

A disciple's focus should not only be about fruit, but that fruit remain.

CONCLUSION 5

What must I do to be more productive for Jesus?

What do I need to do to abide more in Jesus?

Have I lost my saltiness?

THE DISCIPLES CONCLUSION

Dear Lord,

Let me be an instrument used by You to bear more fruit for Your kingdom. Take away the spirit of being satisfied with some fruit. Purge me as You will. Remove all the things that hinder me from bearing fruit. Please do not remove me away from Your purpose and plan.

Amen

CONCLUSION 5

CONCLUSION

Must Have Passion

"By this shall all men know that ye are my disciple, if ye have love one to another."
John 13:35

As we look at passion, I believe it should be motivated by one word: "love." What bought our redemption was a strong passion found in the agape love of God. John 3:16 says, *"For God so loved the world, that he gave his only begotten Son, that whosoever believeth in him should not perish, but have everlasting life."* The love Jesus had for a lost and dying world is the love every disciple must possess. We cannot separate love from our lives or Christian walk, because it is the defining point that describes our relationship with Jesus Christ. In this way people will know we are Jesus' disciples by more than our possessions, talents, or gifts of the Spirit. They will know by the love that we show not only to the church, our families, and our communities but also our love toward our enemies.

"A new command I give you: Love one another. As I have loved you, so you must love one another. By this everyone will know that you are my disciples, if you love one another." (John 14:34, 35)

By our love, people can see and understand the connection we have with Jesus. Love is not an option, but a commandment from God. Our lives are ordered by the love of a Father. Many disciples confuse Jesus' commandment to love with like. There are many people I love but I don't necessary like their attitude, personality, or their approach on matters.

I can love them and not care for how they operate. Another confusion is love and agreement. Some feel if I love them I agree with their actions... but this is not true. Jesus loves us and never agrees with all of our actions.

We are called to love everyone... even the so-called person who seems to be unlovable. We are not given the opportunity to select persons to love and persons not to love. Oftentimes, our love is only the result of someone's love or care for us. We know this cannot be the rule for disciples. Jesus commands us to love even our enemies. Jesus says it is easy to love someone who loves you. The true sign of a disciple: To love according to scriptures. The disciple's real challenge is not only to love their enemies but also to pray and do good to them. Jesus states in Matthew 5:43-48:

"Ye have heard that it hath been said, Thou shalt love thy neighbour, and hate thine enemy. But I say unto

you, Love your enemies, bless them that curse you, do good to them that hate you, and pray for them which despitefully use you, and persecute you; That ye may be the children of your Father which is in heaven: for he maketh his sun to rise on the evil and on the good, and sendeth rain on the just and on the unjust. For if ye love them which love you, what reward have ye? do not even the publicans the same? And if ye salute your brethren only, what do ye more than others? do not even the publicans so?"

We as disciples must stand out from the world. The world teaches us to take matters into our own hands; to get an eye for an eye, and to seek revenge. God teaches otherwise; we are to trust in Him. Disciples trust God to be with them even when it seems like their enemies are winning. Disciples must remember vengeance belongs to God.

"Dearly beloved, avenge not yourselves, but rather give place unto wrath: for it is written, Vengeance is mine; I will repay, saith the Lord." (Romans 12:19)

Our love for Jesus can never be compromised with the world. Our connection of this world must be very loose. When we start putting too much love in the world; we begin claiming our treasure in the world. Always keep in mind that we are in this world, but not of this world. Jesus says when we actually love this world, the love of Father is not present in the life of the disciple.

"Love not the world, neither the things that are in the world. If any man love the world, the love of the Father is not in him. For all that is in the world, the lust of the flesh, and the lust of the eyes, and the pride of life, is not of the Father, but is of the world." (I John 2:15-16)

The love of this will distract our focus as disciples. When we start loving something, it is almost natural to want to serve what we love. "We cannot serve God and the world." (Matthew 6:24)

We are to love God with everything we have. This love supersedes all other stereotypes and beliefs. Our love for Jesus fuels our passion. When we love Jesus right, we become passionate about His passion: souls.

CONCLUSION 6

Who have you I placed on the un-love list of my life because of unforgiveness? Do they have a relationship with Jesus?

Do I always practice unconditional love?

Is my love tank empty?

THE DISCIPLES CONCLUSION

Dear Lord,

Thank You for loving me when I was unloveable. Thank You for continuously loving me through my failures and my mistakes. Help me to love as You do (with no motive or reason). Give me the unconditional love that will change lives for Your Kingdom. For those who want to cause harm to me, help me to love and forgive. Remove any grudges or hatred I have for anyone.

Amen

CONCLUSION 6

CONCLUSION 7

Must Know His Position

"The disciple is not above his master, nor the servant above his lord."
Matthew 10:24

The success and effectiveness of ministry rise and fall on the understanding of roles. This is so clear in the function of the Godhead or the Holy Trinity. God the Father was the creator of the plan. God the Son was the redeemer of the plan. God the Holy Spirit was the executer of the plan. Each person of the Holy Trinity operated in their role to fulfill the plan of redemption for mankind.

THE DISCIPLES CONCLUSION

The role as a disciple is a servant, and Jesus is the Master. There should never be any confusion about these two roles. We know that Jesus is never confused about His role in our lives. Where the problem usually lies is when we try to be the master, instead of the servant. When we say "Jesus is the master of our lives," we are saying He has complete authority and sovereignty over us. When we mix the roles of master and servant, the result can be moving in the wrong direction: we miss the Voice of God; we speak things God never said; and we lead people astray from God.

A disciple must understand he doesn't have enough wisdom or control to be the Master. Our life's experiences are limited. A statement that was used in my military career and has stayed with me is "stay in your lane." When one tries to be the master; he messes things up, and then looks for Jesus to clean up.

CONCLUSION 7

In our role as a disciple (servant), we are all students of the Holy Spirit. We must allow the Holy Spirit to guide our lives, so we can be faithful servants to Jesus Christ. God will call the faithful servant out. Matthew 25:33 says, *"His lord said unto him, 'Well done, good and faithful servant; thou hast been faithful over a few things, I will make thee ruler over many things: enter thou into the joy of thy lord.'"* It is impossible to be faithful to Jesus Christ, the Master, when the disciple is trying to dictate the role of the master. It is easy to be out of God's will when one tries to play the role of the master.

One thing I have found in following the Master, when times are going well, it is easy to let Jesus be in charge. But the moment I am faced with a circumstance, I want to take over the circumstance.

The Master is always watching. Our actions are constantly before His Eyes. A disciple should live his life as if he can physically see the Master every second of the day. When we make Jesus the Master of our lives, we are allowing Him to be Lord of our lives. Many Christians do not have a problem with the Savior part of Jesus, because everyone wants to be saved from something. But Jesus being Lord means He has complete control over our jobs, families, monies, relationships, and daily walk with Him. To be a disciple of Jesus, we should be humble, obedient, ready, and always honor the Master.

When Jesus is allowed to be the master and we are the servants, we say to God, "I am willing to live under authority." Disciples must live under authority. If a disciple cannot live under the authority of Jesus, it will be difficult to live under authority in other areas of his life. The result of not living under authority is a disciple living a complicated life, which leads to living out of order.

In what areas of my life am I still trying to be the Master?

What is my role as a servant to Jesus Christ?

Have I stepped into the Master's lane today?

THE DISCIPLES CONCLUSION

Dear Lord,

I pray for a humble heart, and that I will be the best servant with the help of the Holy Spirit. Please remind me of my role in building Your Kingdom. Teach me to always have honor and reverence for Your position.

Amen

CONCLUSION 7

CONCLUSION

Must Be Willing To Press

Then said Jesus to those Jews which believed on Him, "If ye continue in my word, then are ye my disciples indeed."
John 8:31

In order for a disciple to remain the person God has called him to be, he must press into the Word of God. The Word of God has been given to us so we can live by all of its contents. As a disciple, the Word of God is the tool that guides, strengthens, and encourages. The Word of God is truth. In John 17:17, Jesus says, *"Sanctify them through thy truth: thy word is truth."* For disciples, the Word of God is our rulebook for Christian living. The Word is the full inspiration of God. It is our profit and gain in life. Let's look at Paul and how he addresses the use of God's Word in 2 Timothy 3:16, 17:

"All scripture is given by inspiration of God, and is profitable for doctrine, for reproof, for correction, for instruction in righteousness: That the man of God may be perfect, thoroughly furnished unto all good works."

Paul identifies the authority and the validity of God's Word. What makes the Word so powerful is that it is inspired by God, meaning "God breathed." The entire Word is inspired by God, the parts you agree with and the parts you don't. In other words, the verses you choose to implement in your life and the ones you choose to ignore is still God-breathed. Paul provided five benefits of pressing into the Word.

Benefit #1—Doctrine
Doctrine reminds the disciple what he believes. As a disciple, we must know what we

believe and stand on what we believe. What we believe is all we have in this Christian walk.

Benefit #2—Reproof

Reproof reminds the disciple what is wrong. The Word of God identifies and makes very clear what is right and/or wrong in our lives. The Word of God answers your questions of what to do in all situations.

Benefit #3—Correction

Correction reminds the disciple how to correct the wrong. God's Word reveals the wrong and leads us to the path of righteousness. If a disciple is wrong, he must come back to the Word to find the light.

Benefit #4—Instruction in righteousness

Instruction in righteousness reminds a disciple how to live righteously. The Word of God gives the disciple clear direction on how to live the life that honors God.

Benefit #5—Thoroughly furnished

Thoroughly furnished reminds the disciple that he is fully equipped to do all that God wants him to do. God's Word properly applied and used will give the disciple what is needed for life and Kingdom building.

With all that has been presented, the Word of God cannot be just a casual read, but it must become who we are. God's Word is always available. The disciple understands that the Word of God is true, powerful, inspired, and supersedes any other words written. The Word of God equips the disciple for ministry. The most effective tool in the life of a disciple is the Word of God. The Word is powerful. Hebrews 4:12 reads, *"For the word of God is quick, and powerful, and sharper than any twoedged sword, piercing even to the dividing asunder of soul and spirit, and of the joints and marrow, and is a discerner of the thoughts and intents of the heart."* The Word of God will identify who we are in every assignment and circumstance.

The key to successfully living on this earth, as a disciple, is pressing into the Word of God. The Holy Spirit and time will help the disciple in fulfilling his assignment. Jesus uses clear words. He says that the disciple must continue. In other words, the disciple must remain in the Word of God. God's Word helps us to understand God better (even with our finite minds). The more a disciple presses into the Word, the more it will dictate the disciple's power, influence and effectiveness in Kingdom building. The strength of a disciple is in the Word of God.

The Word of God keeps the disciple connected. This connectivity is important in the maturity of a disciple. Even the world understands the importance of connectivity, and does not care if it is positive or negative. Jesus says continue in the Word. What we are connected to will drain or fill; withdraw or deposit; and break or make us.

Remaining hungry for the Word of God will keep the disciple seeking and desiring more of God. God makes a promise: if we stay hungry, we will be filled. Matthew 5:6 says, *"Blessed are they which do hunger and thirst after righteousness: for they shall be filled."* When we lose our appetite for something, most of the time, we stop eating it. If we lose our appetite for the Word, we will stop pressing into it. We would settle for the minimum. A disciple cannot afford to lose his appetite for the spiritual food provided in the Word of God.

CONCLUSION 8

Have I lost the hunger for God's Word?

Does the Word of God truly guide my life?

What must I do to increase my time in the Word of God?

Dear Lord,

I want to not only read Your Word, but I want to be an example of Your Word. Renew my hunger and thirst for Your Word. I pray to always let the Word be a lamp to my feet and a light to my path. Let Your Word rain in my heart always.

Amen

CONCLUSION 8

CONCLUSION

Must be Prepared to Forgive

"For if ye forgive men their trespasses, your heavenly Father will also forgive you:"
Matthew 6:14

We live in a world full of unforgiveness. We learn from the world's standards to hold on to certain things, whether positive or negative. I consider unforgiveness as unneeded luggage that we carry around. Hebrews 12:1 says, *"...let us lay aside every weight and the sin which doth so easily beset us, and let us run with patience the race that is set before us."* I believe one of those weights the writer is speaking of is unforgiveness. A disciple is a target for friendly and enemy fire. Nothing happens to a disciple that is beyond forgiveness. Unforgiveness left unattended will cause the disciple: (1) to be a stumbling block; (2) to have hindered prayers; and (3) to be in bondage. When unforgiveness is in the heart of the disciple, he is no longer free. He will be constantly connected to anger, resentment, and (sometimes) hatred. A disciple must find a way to forgive. Just because the disciple is called to forgive doesn't mean this will be an easy task.

There are two very difficult hurts that are common among Christians and both are very hard to get over and/or recover.

- Church Hurt
- Family Hurt

A disciple must forgive if he wants forgiveness, and to have his sacrifice received by God. Jesus says in Matthew 6:14, *"For if ye forgive men their trespasses, your heavenly Father will also forgive you."* Jesus also says in Matthew 5:23, 24 *"Therefore if thou bring thy gift to the altar, and there rememberest that thy brother hath ought against thee; Leave there thy gift before the altar, and go thy way; first be reconciled to thy brother, and then come and offer thy gift."* The real sense of unforgiveness is the evidence of the lack of trust in God.

There are countless reasons why one may not forgive:

- Pain (emotional, physical, or mental)
- The offender has moved on with his/her life
- Lack of apology
- Empty apology
- Loss (person or possessions)
- Refusal
- Insecurity
- Remembering the act

THE DISCIPLES CONCLUSION

Jesus set the standard for forgiveness in Matthew 18:21. Peter asked Jesus how often one should forgive a person that offends him. Jesus responded *"...seventy times seven"* (Matthew 18:22). What Jesus was really saying is that we are not to keep a record of anyone's offense towards us.

As a disciple, we cannot afford to hold unforgiveness. Unforgiveness becomes a hindrance to the ministry and life of a disciple. Forgiveness is not an option; it is a commandment of God. The disciple must choose to forgive, and release his right to get even. God will fight for the disciple and avenge him for justice (Romans 12:19).

Jesus gives clear instructions on how we approach those that curse, hate or persecute us. We are to love and pray for them.

"But I say unto you, "Love your enemies, bless them that curse you, do good to them that hate you, and pray for them which despitefully use you, and persecute you;" For if ye love them which love you, what reward have ye? do not even the publicans the same?" (Matthew 5:44, 46)

No matter how one hurts you; God takes it very seriously when we do not forgive. If you choose not to forgive, you are keeping yourself in disobedience and bondage. Let's look at the parable Jesus gives about forgiveness:

"Therefore is the kingdom of heaven likened unto a certain king, which would take account of his servants. And when he had begun to reckon, one was brought unto him, which owed him ten thousand talents. But forasmuch as he had not to pay, his lord commanded him to be sold, and his wife, and children, and all that he had, and payment to be made. The servant therefore fell down, and worshipped him, saying, Lord, have patience with me, and I will pay thee all. Then the lord of that servant

was moved with compassion, and loosed him, and forgave him the debt. But the same servant went out, and found one of his fellowservants, which owed him an hundred pence: and he laid hands on him, and took him by the throat, saying, Pay me that thou owest. And his fellowservant fell down at his feet, and besought him, saying, Have patience with me, and I will pay thee all. And he would not: but went and cast him into prison, till he should pay the debt. So when his fellowservants saw what was done, they were very sorry, and came and told unto their lord all that was done. Then his lord, after that he had called him, said unto him, O thou wicked servant, I forgave thee all that debt, because thou desiredst me: Shouldest not thou also have had compassion on thy fellowservant, even as I had pity on thee? And his lord was wroth, and delivered him to the tormentors, till he should pay all that was due unto him. So likewise shall my heavenly Father do also unto you, if ye from your hearts forgive not everyone his brother their trespasses." (Matthew 18:23-35)

This parable explains how a servant (with a hopeless situation) had a tremendous amount of debt owed to a king. This debt could not be paid in several lifetimes. The king ordered that the servant and family be sold for payment of his debt, but the servant pleaded openly to the king for mercy. The king moved with compassion forgave the servant. Would you believe, this same servant had the audacity to cast a fellow servant into prison? He found and confronted a person who owed him literally pennies compared to his debt to the king. The poor man begged for mercy, but the servant ignored his plea.

This parable does not sound real, but it is an example of how we are when we do not forgive. We had a debt that we could never repay. But because God sent His only Son (John 3:16), our debt was paid. There is no offense too large for us to forgive. Forgiveness is a sign of maturity and growth as a disciple.

THE DISCIPLES CONCLUSION

Do I have any unforgiveness in my heart?

Do I have limits to my forgiveness?

Am I selective when it comes to forgiveness?

CONCLUSION 9

Dear Lord,

Thank You for the forgiveness You provided me by sacrificing Your Life on the cross. Help me to always forgive no matter what the offense may be. Please cleanse my heart of any unforgiveness.

Amen

THE DISCIPLES CONCLUSION

CONCLUSION

Must Be One of Prayer

"And he spake a parable unto them to this end, that men ought always to pray, and not to faint."
Luke 18:1

A disciple does not only pray, but also has a lifestyle of prayer. For the disciple, spending time with God is crucial and necessary. Prayer should not be a last resort; it is the disciple's only resort. Prayer is communication between God and the disciple. Prayer is not just a monologue to God by the disciple, but a dialogue with Him. God talks to the disciple. The most spiritual discipline that a disciple can participate in is prayer. Prayer is the key to the blessings, power, and influence of God.

The enemy wants to distract us from spending time in prayer. The enemy will do anything to keep us from prayer. Prayer penetrates and defeats darkness. It moves the Hand of God. Prayer is the door to the blessings of God. Prayer keeps the connection between God and the disciple.

Some keys to an effective prayer life are:

(1) Praying God's Word
(2) Praying Consistently
(3) Praying in the Spirit
(4) Praying with Anticipation
(5) Praying with Passion

CONCLUSION 10

1. *Praying God's Word*

God responds to His Word, and His Word is already established. God blesses according to His Word. God will answer the prayers in your life based on His Word. God is waiting for a disciple to declare His Word, so He can fulfill it. Then said the LORD unto me, *"Thou hast well seen: for I will hasten my word to perform it."* (Jeremiah 1:12)

When God's Word goes forward, it shall fulfill its destination. The disciple must believe that God will not say anything He won't carry out. *"So shall my word be that goeth forth out of my mouth: it shall not return unto me void, but it shall accomplish that which I please, and it shall prosper in the thing whereto I sent it."* (Isaiah 55:11)

2. Praying Consistently

The disciples must be consistent in prayer. Life of consistency in prayer keeps us closer to God. When we are consistent in prayer, it leaves less room for doubt and the work of Satan in our thoughts. The Apostle Paul declared in 1 Thessalonians 5:17 *"Pray without ceasing."* Colossians 4:2 says, *"Continue in prayer, and watch in the same with thanksgiving."*

3. Praying in the Spirit

Disciples must trust, lean, and depend on the Holy Spirit. The Holy Spirit knows more about our needs than we do. The Holy Spirit knows the deep things of our Father (1 Corinthians 2:11). The Holy Spirit was given to us to be our helper and counselor. The Holy Spirit prays for us. Romans 8:26 says, "Likewise the Spirit also helpeth our infirmities: for we know not what we should pray for as we ought: but the Spirit itself maketh intercession for us with groanings which cannot be uttered."

4. *Praying with Anticipation*

When the disciple prays, he must believe and be in anticipation of God's response. Hebrews 11:6 says, *"But without faith it is impossible to please him: for he that cometh to God must believe that he is, and that he is a rewarder of them that diligently seek him."* It is important that the disciple aligns his prayers with the Heart of God.

5. *Praying with Passion*

When the disciple comes to God in prayer, he should give the Father all he has. A prayer with passion releases worry. It comes humbly to God; and it expresses sincere thanksgiving for God. Paul said it this way, *"Be careful for nothing; but in everything by prayer and supplication with thanksgiving let your requests be made known unto God."* (Philippians 4:6)

CONCLUSION 10

Do I have a consistent prayer life?

Do I go to God only when I need Him?

Do I truly trust God when I pray?

THE DISCIPLES CONCLUSION

Dear Lord,

Keep me at Your feet daily, and allow my life to be a life of prayer. Help me to balance my schedule, so that I will have more time with You. Let Your Voice reign in my ears and my heart. Cause me to be deaf to the voices I do not need to hear.

Amen

CONCLUSION 10

CONCLUSION

Must Have Positive Obedience

"If ye love me, keep my commandments."
John 14:15

Obedience will challenge every area of the disciple's life. If there isn't obedience; there isn't a relationship. Our obedience identifies the intimacy we have as a disciple of Jesus. Our obedience determines how much our Father can trust us with Kingdom business. Positive obedience is following through with God's Word.

Signs of disobedience:

The Escape

Running from what God is telling us to do is blatant disobedience. I call it "the Jonah Syndrome". God told Jonah to minister to the people of Nineveh (Jonah 1:1, 2). Jonah's response: "... *rose up to flee unto Tarshish from the presence of the LORD, and went down to Joppa; and he found a ship going to Tarshish: so he paid the fare thereof, and went down into it, to go with them unto Tarshish from the presence of the LORD.*" (verse 3)

Jonah intentionally ran from the Presence and Instruction of God. There isn't a way a disciple can be obedient to God if he runs away from Him.

The Exchange

The exchange is when the disciple uses the Word of God, incorrectly. He tries to maneuver in his situation to do what he feels is right. When we try to adjust God's Word, we are saying: "God, Your plan is not good enough for me. I have a better plan." I believe a disciple should be challenged in his walk with Jesus. When one does things that are always comfortable or easy, it can lead to destruction and separation from God. When a disciple cultivates in God's Word, he will be challenged by the Spirit. His spiritual growth and relationship will prosper.

The Exclusion

Exclusion is when the disciple omits parts of God's Word and obeys another part. Some calls this selective or partial obedience. We understand that God is very specific. When God gives instructions, He expects them to be carried out to the letter. God gave specific instructions to Noah in the building of the ark for the flood. Noah was not to deviate from any of God's instructions. As it pertains to the building of the Tabernacle, God was specific with Moses in Exodus 25:9, *"According to all that I shew thee, after the pattern of the tabernacle, and the pattern of all the instruments thereof, even so shall ye make it."* The Tabernacle was God's dwelling place.

Disciples of Jesus Christ cannot pick and choose what they will obey. All of God's plans, words, and assignments must always be obeyed. When we obey God, we are saying "I trust Him even when I don't see, hear, or feel Him in any situation." Oftentimes the disciple does not understand that his obedience is connected with his faith in God. Quite often, disobedience takes place when we don't trust enough to follow and obey God's Word.

The disciple must remember God's Ways and Thoughts are not the same as his. The disciple must embrace the words found in Isaiah 55:8-9:

"For my thoughts are not your thoughts, neither are your ways my ways, saith the LORD. For as the heav-

ens are higher than the earth, so are my ways higher than your ways, and my thoughts than your thoughts."

When one has positive obedience, he is building a strong foundation that will last through a storm. Obedience is the mechanism needed in good or bad times. When we obey God's Word, our obedience sets us up for a successful battle. Jesus provides two different responses to the Word and the results are different as well. Matthew 7:24-27:

"Therefore whosoever heareth these sayings of mine, and doeth them, I will liken him unto a wise man, which built his house upon a rock: And the rain descended, and the floods came, and the winds blew, and beat upon that house; and it fell not: for it was founded upon a rock. And every one that heareth these sayings of mine, and doeth them not, shall be likened unto a foolish man, which built his house upon the sand: And the rain descended, and the floods came, and the winds blew, and beat upon that house; and it fell: and great was the fall of

it. *And it came to pass, when Jesus had ended these sayings, the people were astonished at his doctrine."*

I truly believe the conclusion of obedience is in the fact that God would rather have our obedience then, a multitude of sacrifices. First Samuel 15:22 says, *"And Samuel said, 'Hath the LORD as great delight in burnt offerings and sacrifices, as in obeying the voice of the LORD? Behold, to obey is better than sacrifice, and to hearken than the fat of rams.'"* This verse is a response to Saul disobeying God. God told Saul to utterly destroy all the Amalekites and all their possessions (1 Samuel 15:3). Saul destroyed the Amalekites, but kept alive, King Agag and the best livestock. Saul's defense for his disobedience was that he would sacrifice the living livestock unto the Lord. Oftentimes, disciples try to dress up their disobedience with sacrifices (works). God does not want a ritual; He wants an obedient heart.

CONCLUSION 11

Have I substituted sacrifices for obedience? List them.

Am I determined to obey all of God's Word?

Where am I lacking in obedience to the Lord?

Dear Lord,

Let me not be selective in obeying Your Word. Cause me to embrace Your ways and Your thoughts. If there is any seed of disobedience, cleanse it from my heart, mind, mouth, and spirit. Let Your Word have constant reign in my thoughts and decisions.

Amen

CONCLUSION 11

CONCLUSION 12

Must Have a Purged Heart

"Create in me a clean heart, O God; and renew a right spirit within me."
Psalm 51:10

In the natural, the heart is the most important organ in the human body. The heart pumps blood throughout the body. The blood, filled with nutrients and oxygen, helps remove waste from our system. The heart is vital to our lives and how we live.

One may ask the question, "Why is the heart so important to the life of a disciple?" There are many reasons. The heart is the access door to who we are in ministry. One's heart determines what type of disciple he will become. God has ordained that the heart is the path to one becoming a disciple. Romans 10:9, 10 says, *"That if thou shalt confess with thy mouth the Lord Jesus, and shalt believe in thine heart that God hath raised him from the dead, thou shalt be saved. For with the heart man believeth unto righteousness; and with the mouth confession is made unto salvation."*

The heart speaks and identifies who we are in relation to the Kingdom. We understand that our mouth determines what is in the heart. Matthew 12:34 says, *"O generation of vipers, how can ye, being evil, speak good things? for out of the abundance of the heart the mouth speaketh."*

We must understand that everything comes out of the heart. Proverbs 4:23 tells us that the issues of life flows out of the heart. The key to keeping the right heart before God is the work of the Holy Spirit. The Holy Spirit should have free access to the heart of the disciple. This access is so that the Holy Spirit can clean, search, and renew our hearts. The heart is very important to the success of Kingdom ministry. A disciple can only go as far as he will allow the Holy Spirit to lead. Sin contaminates the heart and if left unchecked, it will damage ministry.

The story of David and Bathsheba is a powerful example of this (2 Samuel 11). Once confronted with his sin, David prayed unto the Lord:

"Hide thy face from my sins, and blot out all mine iniquities. Create in me a clean heart, O God; and renew a right spirit within me. Cast me not away from thy presence; and take not thy holy spirit from me. Restore unto me the joy of thy salvation; and uphold me with thy free spirit." (Psalm 51:9-12)

David asks God to do a new work in him, because he allowed himself to fall into sin. A disciple cannot ignore sin in his life; he must address it. David identified that he had a heart problem. If his heart was not fixed, David would find himself committing sin all over again. He knew that his present heart situation would forfeit the Presence of God. David cries out to a mighty God to purge and renew his heart and spirit. Heart problems take away the joy that God gives. This is one of several reasons why God said David was a man after His Own Heart (Acts 13:22).

When a disciple has a purged heart, he is actively involved in:

(1) *Bringing a Hunger for God*

"Blessed are they which do hunger and thirst after righteousness: for they shall be filled." (Matthew 5:6)

(2) *Bringing Worship and Praise towards God*

"*Let everything that hath breath praise the LORD. Praise ye the LORD.*" (Psalm 150:6)

(3) *Bringing Glory to God*

"*Whether therefore ye eat, or drink, or whatsoever ye do, do all to the glory of God.*" (I Corinthians 10:31)

(4) *Bringing an Unclean Heart to God*

"*If I regard iniquity in my heart, the Lord will not hear me.*" (Psalm 66:18)

(5) *Standing Right before God*
"*Who shall ascend into the hill of the LORD? or who shall stand in his holy place?*" (Psalm 24:3)

THE DISCIPLES CONCLUSION

Do I have spiritual heart troubles?

Is my heart growing closer to Jesus daily?

Do I have a purged heart?

CONCLUSION 12

Dear Lord,

I have the same cry as David, *"Create in me a clean heart and renew a right spirit in me."* Open my eyes to see the things You see in my heart. Let my heart always seek to praise, honor, and glorify You. You are the only true and wise God.

Amen

THE DISCIPLES CONCLUSION

CONCLUSION

Must Fulfill the Great Commission

"And Jesus came and spake unto them, saying, "All power is given unto me in heaven and in earth. Go ye therefore, and teach all nations, baptizing them in the name of the Father, and of the Son, and of the Holy Ghost: Teaching them to observe all things whatsoever I have commanded you: and, lo, I am with you always, even unto the end of the world. Amen.""
Matthew 28:18:18-20

The greatest of all role or conclusion must be to intentionally fulfill the words of the Great Commission. It has been said that the Great Commission is the only commission. There isn't a greater act of obedience that can be found in the Words of Jesus. Jesus' work on the cross was done so that the Great Commission could be fulfilled. If we fulfill the first 12 roles, role #13 should be a changed lifestyle.

The greatest work a disciple can do is to help someone come to the saving knowledge of Jesus Christ. The disciple has been promised strength and power from the Holy Spirit. We, as disciples, are called to go out but not in our own strength. After we are filled with the Holy Spirit, we have the responsibility to be witnesses for Jesus Christ. So often in the church, we take ownership of being filled with Holy Spirit to do everything but to fulfill the Great Commission.

"But ye shall receive power, after that the Holy Ghost is come upon you: and ye shall be witnesses unto me both in Jerusalem, and in all Judaea, and in Samaria, and unto the uttermost part of the earth." (Acts 1:8)

CONCLUSION 13

In carrying out the Great Commission, there isn't any deference of persons. We cannot judge or choose the individuals that need to come into the Kingdom. We have one responsibility and that is to preach the Gospel of Jesus Christ.

"And he said unto them, Go ye into all the world, and preach the gospel to every creature." (Mark 16:15)

I truly believe greater numbers would come to the Kingdom, if disciples are not selective when preaching the Gospel to others. A disciple must understand that in order to carry the Gospel in all the world, he must come out of his comfort zone of ministry.

Jesus said John 14:12, *"Verily, verily, I say unto you, he that believeth in me, the works that I do shall he do also, and greater works than these shall he do because I go unto my Father."* The greater works do not mean we are going to out shine Jesus. Jesus was the greatest human to walk the earth. He was without sin. (Hebrews 4:14)

Jesus was one man, but as great of a human being as He was; He could not be at two places at one time. That is why Jesus said that it was expedient that He return to the Father, so the Comforter (the Holy Spirit) could come to help His disciples. (John 16:7)

The Holy Spirit's job is to help us fulfill the Great Commission. The Holy Spirit helps the church (Body of Christ) to do greater works. To be a witness is the task of every disciple.

CONCLUSION 13

What will I do with the Words of Jesus?

Is the Great Commission my personal mission?

Have I witnessed the Gospel of Jesus Christ to someone today (this week; this month; this year)?

Dear Lord,

Help me to have the appetite to fulfill the Great Commission. Holy Spirit, please burden my heart for lost souls. Let sharing the Gospel of Jesus Christ be my daily agenda.

Amen

About the Author

DR. AARON R. JONES is a native Washingtonian. He is the Senior Pastor of the New Hope Church of God in Waldorf, MD. He currently serves as the District Overseer of the DELMARVA DC District. He also serves a Chaplain for the Charles County Sheriff's Office and is a retired Army Chaplain.

Dr. Jones is the author of six additional books entitled: *How the Holy Trinity Communicates to Mankind, Eight Effective Keys to Personal Evangelism, The Pastor's Intercessor, Out of My Comfort Zone to Worship God,* and *Joshua's Resolution.*

Dr. Jones is happily married to Rev. Sharon Jones of 18 years.

www.ingramcontent.com/pod-product-compliance
Lightning Source LLC
Chambersburg PA
CBHW072051290426
44110CB00014B/1636